The Perfect Growth Formula
A balanced approach to growing
your business without stress or strain.

William S. Mattern and Gregory S. Chambers

Copyright © 2017 William S. Mattern and Gregory S. Chambers

All rights reserved.

ISBN: 1548374989
ISBN-13: 978-1548374983

"Growth is never by mere chance;
it is the result of forces working together."
– James Cash Penney

CONTENTS

	QUOTATION	
1	WHAT IS THE PERFECT GROWTH FORMULA?	1
2	INBOUND	3
3	OUTREACH	7
4	DATA	11
5	BEING OUT OF BALANCE	15
6	PUTTING IT ALL TOGETHER	19
7	FINAL THOUGHTS	21
8	THE PERFECT GROWTH FORMULA SELF-ASSESSMENT	23
	ABOUT THE AUTHORS	

THE PERFECT GROWTH FORMULA

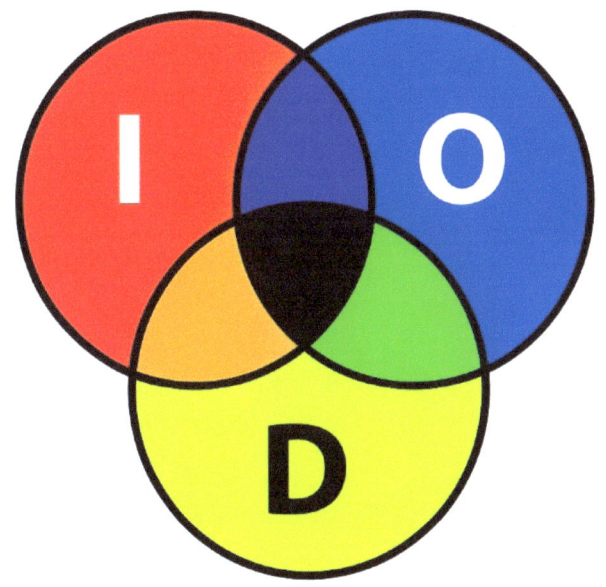

1. WHAT IS THE PERFECT GROWTH FORMULA?

The first question usually asked about the perfect growth formula is where did this come from?

Clients are surprised to learn that it came almost entirely from them. We combined their experiences with the strategies and tactics GoLeads employs in regard to how we generate new business. The more we looked at how we've grown our business in the last seventeen years, how our customers are growing their business, and even how prospects told us they hoped to grow their business, the Growth Formula began to emerge. It is the world that not only GoLeads is living in, but the majority of our very best customers are living in too.

Referring to the graphic, the way we started in the world of marketing can be found on the outreach side of the equation or the big yellow circle. As time went on, we focused more on the inbound circle, where we tried to get customers to come to us (the big red circle). Both of those activities generated lots of sales, but even more semi-interested prospects and tons of data. That is where the blue circle, Data, comes in. To leverage all that information we use analytics to learn more about these prospects and customers. We used that information to direct our marketing and even take that information to our customers, asking for referrals. This learning loop gave us insights that made us more valuable to prospects and also made it easier to reconnect. As time went by, we found that we aren't the only company engaged in these activities looking for tools and help. This realization led to the Growth Formula—an easy way to explain what we're doing to anyone trying to grow their business using the same tools.

Let's jump into the first part of the equation. Inbound.

THE PERFECT GROWTH FORMULA

2. INBOUND

We have a simple definition of inbound: getting customers to call us. It could be future customers calling us, qualified prospects calling us, or anyone else who needs our services or products finding us. Today, the way we make this happen is to be where our customers can find us on the internet, and then direct that traffic to our website. That's our primary goal–make sure our website is being found.

The reason for this is simple: a lot of our potential prospects are on the internet, using search engines to do research about the very problems we solve. Some are even far enough in their search to look for the products and services we provide by name. Our goal is to maximize the amount of that traffic that ends up on our website. This is achieved in a number of ways—pay-per-click ads using tools like AdWords, press releases, writing articles, and more. We are open to placing anything on our online properties that will enhance our website and increase its chances of answering a question our clients ask the search engines. In other words, anything that will increase our online visibility.

This focus on being where our prospects are searching transformed our business fifteen years ago. Today, even though online marketing has become more complicated, what hasn't changed is the fact that it's good to be visible during online searches. And everyone agrees that it's good to have qualified prospects finding you, and keeping your sales people from having to engage in a lengthy sales cycle. Our reps are human, and in the end, nobody really likes making 100 interrupting phone calls a day. Especially when the alternative is getting a qualified prospect to call them, and say, "Hey, you have this product, right?" What salesperson wouldn't want that?

To make this happen, we are leveraging the website, leveraging the search engines, and making our products and services visible to customers.

Let's talk about how we can help you do the same.

First, when we start looking at a client's website, there are times it feels like the client built their website because one day somebody walked in and said, "Hey, business, you need to get a website." That's not where we want you to start. We want to discern, for this particular business and their customers, the purpose of their website. Unfortunately, it is not Field of Dreams; just because you have it, doesn't mean people will come, even today.

We start by considering what has to happen to make their website visible to prospects. What do we need to do to make sure that website is front and center on the result pages of the major search engines when a prospect searches for information related to the problems our client is solving? To increase visibility, we create content, we increase activity on social media and we invest in pay-per-click advertising like Google AdWords.

We know what you're thinking, "pay-per-click?"

If you sell a complicated product or service, pay-per-click is a great way to get immediate feedback from likely prospects who are typing something into Google. If your ad campaign's keyword phrases are a match and your ad shows up, you can collect that information and learn more about what your future customers are actually searching for. And believe me, what you think they'd search for and what they actually search for are rarely the same thing.

As you know if you've tried paid ads in the past, it can get expensive. Especially if you are advertising using phrases that are early in a prospect's buying cycle. Therefore, once we learn what our prospects are searching for, we focus on making sure the search engine knows our client has the answers to that query. We do this by creating content and using linking strategies to get to the top of the natural search results. Typically referred to as organic traffic, we employ a little science, a little focused effort, and a lot of basic blocking and tackling to earn a spot at the top of page one. Once you can be found in the top results, you're there 24/7. What's best, you don't have to pay for that impression or for getting that prospect to click on your website.

The most impressive inbound example is Amazon. Right? It feels like no matter what product or service you type into a search engine, Amazon shows up in the first three or four spots in that organic search. If Amazon sells it, and the search engine thinks you want it, they're going to direct you to Amazon. It's in the search engine's best interest to do so because the better search results, the more likely you will continue to use that search engine.

Consider this, with services like Amazon Echo and Google Home becoming more and more prevalent, your interaction with a search engine is like talking to a vase. The answers that Alexa gives? They are the top results from the search engines or the organic results. At some point in the future, this will drift into business-to-business transactions too.

Be ready. Today's advantage is tomorrow's assumption.

Lastly, consider the example of GoLeads. There's a good chance that if you're reading this booklet, you initially found us online through a search. That is inbound marketing.

3. OUTREACH

Outreach is best understood as traditional marketing and sales. It's where we actively reach out to the prospect, in contrast to waiting for the prospect to contact us. Think face-to-face office visits, direct mail and telemarketing. While it is all relative, the newest tactics that businesses have implemented surround email marketing, SMS text marketing, and even-account based marketing where we push ads out based on IP addresses and other registered online activity. While the newest tactics are borderline creepy, what all these examples have in common is that they involve reaching out to customers. Or to put it another way; we are finding customers instead of customers finding us.

Although we led this booklet with inbound, we know that most of our clients rely on outreach to generate much of their new business activity. If there are any drawbacks compared to inbound marketing, it's that outreach is a lengthy sales cycle, and any attempts to speed up the buyer's decision leads to margin compression. In other words, discounts or price matching. However, that doesn't happen every time, and overall, prospecting in a traditional format is incredibly valuable. It's just when you have all of the elements of the Perfect Growth Formula working together—inbound, outbound and leveraging your customer base—margins tend to be healthier and discounting less frequent. We'll cover getting all elements working together in coming chapters, but for now, let's focus on outreach.

The number one reason everyone should be using outreach tactics is because of one thing: market penetration. You start with sizing up the entire market, then determine your percentage of penetration. Literally, out of this entire universe of people who can purchase our products and services, how many customers do we currently have? Let's go out and connect with everyone else. In the Growth Formula we take that a step further and combine it with inbound by saying, let's reach them and inspire them to call us back. The way we do get them to call is through telemarketing, direct mail, knocking on doors, and a variety of other tactics whether it's targeting consumers or reaching businesses.

We don't want to "reach out" to just anyone, though. In our definition of outreach, we use as much market information as we can find in order to make each touch more valuable. For example, instead of doing a postcard drop to an entire zip code or set of carrier routes, we do a customer analyzer or a best prospect analyzer and target our outreach very specifically. Once we've identified a set of look-a-like prospects, we start testing. We'll test 500 leads, or maybe 1,000 leads. We'll group them and leave a specific message for this group then test it against a similar message to another group. We're trying to learn what works best. A classic A-B test. We aren't afraid of spending a little bit of money up front as long as the test gives us the marketing intelligence we need to justify a larger investment in the future that is capable of generating long-term sales growth.

For the most part, most companies already are doing some part of outreach marketing—either through telemarketing, on-site visits by salespeople or direct mail.

The newer tactics include email, especially on the B2B side. The results depend heavily on who is on the prspect list, what is being offered and how closely the two are aligned. We focus on the subject line, then the text preview, then the text only email, then the image, then the call-to-action. Email can help you find the "low hanging fruit," but mostly it helps you create equity in your brand, and over time it can help move prospects through their decision-making process.

Not only is the decision a process, but so is email marketing and all of outreach. It takes time but it works.

With many industries, products, and services, outreach is the primary way to build demand. It works, so it makes sense to keep that the primary marketing or sales focus.

We've covered inbound, and we've covered outbound. Next is data.

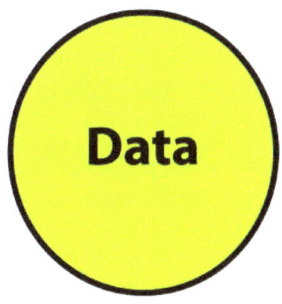

4. DATA

Data is our last group in the Perfect Growth Formula. In our opinion, it's a group that is often overlooked when it comes to new business development, because it holds all the people and organizations that we marketed to in the past. It includes our database of customers–the group that has already paid us–but it also includes those prospects whom we have spoken with but who have never bought from us. For our marketing and sales efforts to produce the best results from the least effort, we use the Data bucket to hold everything together.

The way we approach this is through analytics. We take all the information we've collected on customers, past customers and prospects, and we focus on connecting, educating and inspiring them to work with us in a deeper way. We want to connect with everyone in our database and deepen the conversation.

This doesn't mean we're continuously pounding the database with sales messages, but rather we provide them with information they need to make good decisions in the future, whether it's with us or someone else. If we approach these people in the right way, they allow us to educate them, and hopefully, over time, they are inspired to act. When they are ready to act, we are there via our inbound efforts and we benefit from name recognition. Our company benefits from familiarity or we are in front of them at the right time.

This step is the glue. Actually, it's an incredibly important piece of the equation for a few reasons. First, we have spent the money on capturing the new customer or introducing ourselves to the prospect either by direct investment in advertising or indirect investments with our people and process. If we only start the conversation with prospects and customers without analyzing the results and re-approaching that database, our cost of sales is high. We are recommending you invest in learning from the results you're generating.

The second reason is that we do have some sort of relationship. It may not be a strong relationship, but all relationships start somewhere. If we are not taking advantage of this loose network of people who know of us or have bought from us, we are missing part of the puzzle. Something may happen in a month, something may happen in a year, and sometimes it may take even longer. When answering the question, is it better to be good or to be present, we always default to it being better to being present.

This means that in our database, we have people who have invested tens of thousands of dollars a year with us, but we also have a group who has not paid us a dime, and that's okay. When they are ready, they are ready and we want to be there.

The way we do this starts with three terms we repeat often at GoLeads: we want to connect, educate, and inspire. To connect means we don't always want to be selling. We want to make a connection that establishes a common language and a common understanding of what we're trying to accomplish. To educate means that we want to help prospects and clients like they were friends asking, "If you were me, what would you do?" There are many paths to a solution, which one would you choose? If we can download our experiences and knowledge to our clients and prospects, we are adding value. And to inspire means that if a prospect has never considered a particular solution or encountered a certain problem, we want to be the ones that enlighten that prospect because there's a chance they will turn to us when they need help or want to accomplish a particular goal.

We combine all of this information on the inbound, the outreach, and past experiences and analyze it to get a picture of what the full market potential is. How many customers do I have in this vertical? What's the total market of this vertical? What's my ROI? What's my penetration? Are we profitable in this niche? Do I want to continue to go after this market? It's taking all of our historical sales and marketing work that's been done, bringing it in and analyzing it, then asking, "Where do I go from here?"

We use this information to inform the elements of inbound, outreach, and leveraging data. We make ourselves smarter going forward.

Let's give an example. We have a client that initially asked us for our full database, but it's rare that anyone needs millions of records. They are a magazine publishing company, so we paused that initial request and started by looking at their subscribers. We pulled them in and bumped them up against our databases, everything we had access to, and we did a market analysis and a customer analysis. They had a past responder file too, so we used that to do a prospect analysis.

We had two goals, the first being that we wanted to confirm what their initial guesses were. They knew who they wanted to target based on history and anecdotes, so we tried to put some data behind the hypotheses. Simply confirming that we were on the right path.

The second thing we wanted to accomplish in that analysis is to uncover what we refer to internally as the "Wow" factor. In this case, the wow factor happened when we took a detailed look at their current subscribers. The entire file was over 55 years old. Before the information had been laid out in front of them like that, they had an inkling that their subscribers were aging, but when looking at detailed reports, the director of marketing literally said, "Oh my gosh. We're about to lose our entire . . ." and her voice drifted off. It was dramatic. That's the wow factor.

With the analysis in hand, they called an all hands on deck meeting and said, "We have to talk about this because our subscriber base has aged faster than we thought and there will come a time when they won't need our publication."

That information forced us to rethink the big database rental idea and pay attention to rebuilding the subscriber base for the future. It shaped their strategy going forward. That's the power of leveraging your data.

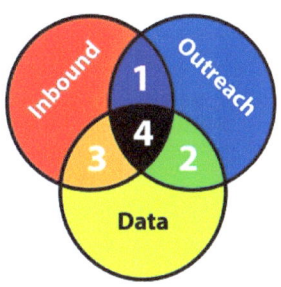

5. BEING OUT OF BALANCE

We've been describing each section of activity in the GoLeads Growth Score individually, but now let's talk about how they all work together. We want all of the sections to be in balance, and the best way to describe why is to take a look at what happens when activities are out of balance.

To keep us on track, we're going to refer to the numbers in the Growth Formula. In balance is number 4. Let's talk about what happens when you have strong inbound activity, strong outbound activity, but you're not leveraging the databases. The most compelling reason for spending time and effort leveraging the customer and prospect database is because you have already spent money attracting that prospect. If you forget about them your cost of sales is too high. You've already made the investment in attracting new customers which means you have a set of prospects who have been exposed to your brand name and solutions. The future cost of sales comes down with each subsequent brand exposure and each add-on product or service your customers purchase.

The questions to ask yourself when someone doesn't buy right away are, "What are our next steps? How do we connect, educate, and inspire over time? How will we keep track of that activity and make sure the initial investment isn't wasted?"

A quick example is a consultant we worked with who used event marketing to meet new business owners, city by city. He was calling in to renew his license with us and happened to catch me on the phone. As we waited for his information to pop-up, I asked if he wanted us to suppress attendees and responders from the last mailing, thinking he had a separate approach with prospects that had responded in some way.

"Why would I do that?" he asked. He described his approach, which was multiple mailings, multiple follow up calls, and an online registration system. I described the work we did with the publishing company, how it might bring down his cost of sales, and it was like I turned on a lightbulb. "Wait, you think I can bring down my costs?" he repeated, and we sketched out a plan on who to re-approach, who to avoid and who to increase the number of touches on. We showed him that his sweet spot is in businesses with over 50 employees, in metropolitan areas (MSAs) 51 through 200, and showed him how to retarget visitors to his registration page.

His results were dramatic. Due in part to our advice, he filled the room twice as fast and was nearly able to eliminate the discounting that occurred the week of the event. It turns out that he used to re-visit cities once a year, but armed with new information from his database, he cut the number of cities he traveled to in half and doubled the number of events.

If your data effort isn't equal to your inbound and outbound effort, you're spending too much on future sales.

What about when inbound is out of balance with outreach and data, number two on the list? To get right to the point, if no one's calling you, internally, we think of you as invisible. You're a best kept secret and the only way someone finds out about you is because of outreach to them. We see this a lot in business-to-business sales. The sales team focuses on making new contacts, outreach, and the marketing team focuses on keeping in touch with them. The rest of the market, others that can benefit from your services or need your product, can't find you.

The big benefit from adding a focus on inbound is that you will shorten your sales cycle. That's because your prospects are helping to qualify themselves. You're not starting at the beginning of the sales cycle, you're starting in the middle. Maybe even close to the end if your materials do a great job of educating the customer.

An example of this happened with a home health care company that worked with families of elderly parents. They sell through a network of advisors and physicians, and came to us looking for an updated list of internal medicine doctors and licensed social workers. They never had a single family contact them directly and assumed it would never happen.

We helped them test a content strategy to get incoming calls. It started with writing a series of articles on the most common questions families had about their services and featured unique answers from their team. We promoted these articles via press releases, links to their website, and teaching staff how to provide pdf versions to families. Within 90 days they started getting calls and questions that we could use to fine-tune the materials. Within 180 days the first leads started coming in. Today this activity accounts for 15 percent of their opportunities and it continues to grow.

Though, if you talk to them today, the leads aren't what they're most impressed with. The most impressive part of the effort is the effect it is having on referrals and recruiting. They found out they really were a best kept secret. Today, their brand name recognition and reputation are on the rise.

Finally, what about number three, an imbalance where the focus is on inbound and data, but there is little to no active outreach? You are leveraging your customer base, and you're getting incoming calls. Why would we need to focus on old fashioned outreach?

The simple answer is that even the best inbound effort won't bring in everybody. We have yet to run into a case where a business has 100 percent market penetration. A customer penetration report will show prospects that work with competitors, that are unaware of the need for your services, or were not in the market before that day. A direct outreach effort to these groups will be easy because you have the materials they need to educate themselves, but they won't find it on their own.

The other benefit we've seen is that businesses that are out of balance with outreach tend to have less ability to forecast more than one or two sales cycles into the future. Are they going to average thirty incoming phone calls this week or will it only be ten? Balancing outreach helps you take control of the market. It makes you less passive.

6. PUTTING IT ALL TOGETHER

When you have all three circles in balance, we say that you are maximizing the results from your sales and marketing efforts. It's a simple idea, but not easy to implement.

Take GoLeads for instance. There are times we can point directly to being out of balance. Whether it's losing people to new opportunities, customer defections, or being distracted by a competitor, it's easy to feel a little wobbly and off-kilter. It's during these times that I find comfort and direction in this graphic. It orients us. It forces us to go back to the basics and think, "Okay, let's fix this. What's our strategy on the inbound side? What's our strategy on the outreach side? How are we leveraging customers?"

This didn't happen overnight. We started this business over fifteen years ago with the strategy that we knew. A full focus on outreach. No one knows us, so we have to get out and start talking to customers. We needed to tell our story.

What was interesting was that fifteen years ago, after creating a website, we kind of stumbled into inbound. We didn't plan on attracting thousands of prospects from online activity, but that is exactly what happened. As you can imagine, once we didn't need to work so hard at outreach, we let it go. As a matter of fact, we became obsessed with getting Google traffic to the detriment of the rest of our marketing and sales efforts. A decade later we looked up and thought, "Is outreach still relative? Is it weird that we sell outreach tools but almost all of our business is coming from inbound?"

Enter the Perfect Growth Formula. This equation allows GoLeads to do a much better job of helping our clients set their own marketing and sales strategies. That's because our clients learn from our experiences—especially the challenges we faced.that come from being out of balance, because that happened to us. We were too out of balance on the inbound side and one day we looked up and the business had leveled off.

It didn't happen all at once. We always have inbound calls coming in but we didn't have anyone reaching out to our database. We didn't have anyone penetrating hot markets directly. We weren't maximizing our growth or maximizing our resources. We're a small business and don't have an Amazon budget, but we want to maximize our sales and marketing spending and we don't want to be afraid to make investments in promising tactics.

The Perfect Growth Formula helped us frame our internal discussions, asking ourselves, "What do we want from our customers? What do we want from our prospects? What are we doing to maximize our effort in each and every area?"

By doing that, a plan emerges effortlessly. It helps us avoid the fate a CEO that I used to work for described when he said, "The absolute worst business is when you have to get new business every single month."

We know what he meant, because we were living it before using the Growth Formula. We started at zero every month, and that caused stress. We wanted more visibility into the pipeline and we looked at ways to find some recurring revenue so we didn't have everything in one basket.

The Perfect Growth Formula forced us, and still forces us, to ask questions about how we want to grow, and the best ways to get the most from our finite resources.

7. FINAL THOUGHTS

This booklet is an overview of the Perfect Growth Formula and it should give you an idea of how your team can use it to frame discussions. This last chapter will answer a few questions that our clients have had when first introduced to the framework.

We've made the claim that the Growth Formula helps with growth, but it goes well beyond that. The way we recommend using it is by throwing the graphic up on the white board and talking about each section, coming up with examples that fit your industry. You'll be surprised with what comes out. For instance, in an early discussion with our sales team, we said, "Here in the Data section, why doesn't someone describe our best customers? Give us some adjectives." And no kidding, we filled up a whiteboard.

Here was the surprising thing, we filled it up with every type of adjective, and what was amazing was that none of the adjectives had anything to do with revenue. None of them were financial. It had everything to do with open, honest, good person, works with me, takes my call, things like that. Only at the very end did somebody speak up and say, "Well, I do like it when they pay."

That's the power of the Growth Formula. It gets your team talking. In that case, we got deep into defining our best customers and asking, "Okay, how do we find those people? Can we mimic them somehow? Can we describe them with data?"

In our case, we decided that the data wasn't deep enough. It just wasn't out there. That forced us to think about tools like this booklet. We needed new ways to find our best customers. We needed to connect with them, educate them to the best of our ability, and then inspire them to take action, letting the results speak for themselves.

It was eye opening for all of us and changed our business.

The last idea we'll leave with you is using the GoLeads Growth Score as a quick assessment tool. The way we suggest that you take the self-assessment is to do it in two steps.

The first step is to ask your team to set a marker for where you are today. Rank yourself on inbound, outbound and data. Use a scale of one to five. One being not so great and five being I don't know how we can get any better.

The second, or follow-up, step is to ask your team where it wants to be. With those two scores in hand, start talking about the best ways to move the needle. The best ways to move from a two to a three in outbound, for instance.

The Perfect Growth Formula is a powerful tool because it's based on what we've learned from our clients. It was developed by combining our clients' experiences with how we at GoLeads generate new business. It also illustrates how we've grown our business in the last fifteen years and where we'd like to take it in the next fifteen years.

Good luck using the framework and if you want to share your experiences please feel free to contact us.

8. PERFECT GROWTH FORMULA SCORING TOOL

To help our sales team assess clients, we developed a scoring tool that assesses any business on two levels. The first is a physical inventory of sales and marketing tools and tactics. The second is a measure of your temperament for growth. Helping answer the questions "Do we have the structure to take advantage of the Growth Formula? And "Do we have the temperament to take advantage of the Growth Formula?"

It should deepen your understanding of the Growth Formula and its direct application to your business. Used correctly, it is designed to generate questions and lively discussion around what you're currently doing and the direction you want to go.

Instructions: There are 36 total questions. Use the scoring system, total your score by section, add up the two section totals, and check the scoring legend at the end.

	QUESTION	SCORING	YOUR SCORE
I-1	Website analytics installed?	0 – No analytics installed 1 – Analytics installed 2 – Analytics, tracking, and landing pages	
I-2	Last social media activity?	0 – No social media 1 – Monthly social media activity 2 – Regular, relevant, activity	
I-3	How many pages are on your site?	0 – Under 50 pages 1 – 100 pages/blog 2 – 200+ pages/blog/downloads	

I-4	Would you rather have new customers or more business from existing customers?	0 – Don't know 1 – Focused on both 2 – We measure all activity, new and existing	
I-5	What is the source of most of your leads?	0 – We have a rough idea 1 – We use last touch attribution 2 – We have a way to measure all touches and weight attribution	
I-6	What is the lead source of most of your sales?	0 – We have a rough idea 1 – We use last touch attribution 2 – We have a way to measure all touches and weight attribution	
		TOTAL for INBOUND	
O-1	Do you have a newsletter or email collection app on your website?	0 – No newsletter, don't email 1 – Semi-regular news sent 2 – Regular email, active segmenting of clients/prospects	
O-2	What is your preferred method of prospecting?	0 – Online only 1 – Mix of online, offline tactics 2 – We use customer profiles, market analysis, active tracking	
O-3	How many prospects do your need to talk to for a sale?	0 – We don't know 1 – Rule of thumb used 2 – Ratio by channel, segmented	
O-4	What does your company do with the non-converting prospects?	0 – Kept in files 1 – Kept in CRM with all prospects 2 – A separate marketing CRM	
O-5	Do you regularly use press releases?	0 – No 1 – On occasion 2 – Regular PR effort	

O-6	How much does it cost to bring in a new customer?	0 – Rough idea 1 – Accounting tracks it 2 – We track and manage Cost per Acquisition (CPA)	
		TOTAL for OUTBOUND	
L-1	Do you have published testimonials on your website?	0 – No published testimonials 1 – Nameless quotes 2 – We have a testimonial strategy	
L-2	Each year, what percentage of your business is repeat business?	0 – Rough idea 1 – Less than 20% is repeat 2 – Over 20%, we have a CRM, and track customer lifetime value	
L-3	What is an expected lifetime value of a new customer?	0 – Rough idea 1 – Accounting tracks it 2 – We track it, track CPA, and measure all activity, inbound and outbound	
L-4	Are your customers local, nationwide, or worldwide?	0 – Rough idea 1 – We have a specific geography 2 – Specific geography, track CPA, and use CRM	
L-5	What customer relationship tool or tools do you use?	0 – Excel 1 – We use a CRM tool 2 – We pull regular detailed reports from our CRM	
		TOTAL for DATA	
		Add Inbound, Outbound, Data scores for TOTAL STRUCTURE for GROWTH Score	

THE PERFECT GROWTH FORMULA

	GROWTH TEMPERAMENT		SCORE
G-1	Our demand is greater than our ability to deliver products or services.	1 Strongly disagree 2 Disagree 3 Agree 4 Strongly Agree	
G-2	Our company has experienced economic ups and downs.	1 Strongly disagree 2 Disagree 3 Agree 4 Strongly Agree	
G-3	We have the right team in place.	1 Strongly disagree 2 Disagree 3 Agree 4 Strongly Agree	
G-4	We have a solid business plan in place.	1 Strongly disagree 2 Disagree 3 Agree 4 Strongly Agree	
G-5	We have capital available to fuel growth.	1 Strongly disagree 2 Disagree 3 Agree 4 Strongly Agree	
		TOTAL for GROWTH	
C-1	We know our customer's purchasing decision process.	1 Strongly disagree 2 Disagree 3 Agree 4 Strongly Agree	
C-2	We conduct regular customer surveys.	1 Strongly disagree 2 Disagree 3 Agree 4 Strongly Agree	
C-3	We know our buyer's reading/media consumption habits.	1 Strongly disagree 2 Disagree 3 Agree 4 Strongly Agree	
C-4	When we first meet prospects, we have to teach them about the problems we solve.	1 Strongly disagree 2 Disagree 3 Agree 4 Strongly Agree	

C-5	Our customers experience fast, early success with our products.	1 Strongly disagree 2 Disagree 3 Agree 4 Strongly Agree	
		TOTAL for CUSTOMER FOCUS	
P-1	We have detailed performance results from past marketing campaigns	1 Strongly disagree 2 Disagree 3 Agree 4 Strongly Agree	
P-2	We encourage experimentation.	1 Strongly disagree 2 Disagree 3 Agree 4 Strongly Agree	
P-3	We consider risk in all planning.	1 Strongly disagree 2 Disagree 3 Agree 4 Strongly Agree	
P-4	We track total sales by time period.	1 Strongly disagree 2 Disagree 3 Agree 4 Strongly Agree	
		TOTAL for HISTORY	
S-1	We have a scalable growth plan in place.	1 Strongly disagree 2 Disagree 3 Agree 4 Strongly Agree	
S-2	We have a clear picture of the company's strengths, weaknesses, and opportunities.	1 Strongly disagree 2 Disagree 3 Agree 4 Strongly Agree	
S-3	Our growth needs to be profitable.	1 Strongly disagree 2 Disagree 3 Agree 4 Strongly Agree	

S-4	Each business unit has its own aims and objectives.	1 Strongly disagree 2 Disagree 3 Agree 4 Strongly Agree	
S-5	We consider multiple options for growth.	1 Strongly disagree 2 Disagree 3 Agree 4 Strongly Agree	
		TOTAL for STRATEGY	
	Add Growth, Customer Focus, History, Strategy scores for TOTAL TEMPERAMENT for GROWTH Score		

SCORING:

The assessment is broken into sections. The first half is focused on your company's growth structure. It's built to answer the question, "If we wanted to put the Perfect Growth Formula to work, are we set up to make it happen?"

GROWTH STRUCTURE TOTAL

Add up your inbound, outbound, and data scores. This is your overall structure score. Out of 34 possible points, a score of 29 to 34 indicates a strong growth structure is in place. You can invest in new growth tactics and your company will be able to measure and manage results. If your score is between 20 and 28, you have some structure in place, but once you put stress on the system, leaks will begin to show which make growth longer and more expensive than it needs to be. Shore up the areas where you scored lowest. If your score is under 20 points, plan your structure before investing heavily in growth tactics.

The assessment is organized into the Growth Formula sections to make it easy for your team to draw up unique strategies that will work for your company.

INBOUND

The first six questions are on inbound structure. If you score between 9-12, your inbound growth structure is great. If you score between 5 and 8, growth pressure will cause some stress in the organization as it tries to keep up. If you score between 0 and 4, before you invest in inbound, focus on structure.

OUTBOUND

The second six questions are around outbound structure. If you score between 9-12, your outbound growth structure is ready for investment. If you score between 5 and 8, growth pressure will cause some stress in the organization as it scrambles to keep up. And if you score between 0 and 4, before you invest in outbound, focus on structure.

DATA

The last set of structure questions are around data structure. If you score between 7-10, your database is ready to be leveraged for growth structure. If you score between 4 and 6, trying to leverage your database for growth will cause organizational stress. And if you score between 0 and 3, before you invest in leveraging your database, focus on structuring the database for analysis.

GROWTH TEMPERAMENT TOTAL

Add up your growth, customer focus, history, and strategy scores. This is your overall growth temperament score. Out of 76 possible points, a score of 68 to 76 indicates that your company has a strong temperament for growth. Coupled with a strong structure score, you are a fighter jet on the tarmac ready to "kick the tires and light the fires." If your score is between 55 and 67, you have some hurdles to overcome in the quest for growth. Start looking in each section and determine where you can shore up the company's temperament as you work on growth. If your score is under 54 points, your company may have the desire to grow, but there are going to be some serious challenges in place. Take a careful look at each section, make plans to improve those areas, and then go back to work on growth.

The separate sections to focus on:

GROWTH

This section's questions (G1-G5) give you an idea on how much experience your company has with growth. A score of 17-20 tells us you have "been there and done that." You're ready for the roller coaster. A score of 12-16 tells us that there may be some challenges ahead and a score of under 12 suggests that your company may answer the question, "why do you want to grow?" with a shrug and a, "why not?"

CUSTOMER FOCUS

This section (C1-C5) shows us how strong your current customer focus is. This is important because thinking like your customer is a key to growth. A score of 17-20 tells us that you are actively embracing the idea that you need to think like your customer, knowing their decision process better than they do. A score of 11-16 suggests that your company is applying energy internally as much as it's applying energy to the customer. It's not a terrible thing, but it limits growth because new opportunities for growing come from the customers, not from internal focus. Score under 10 and you're almost totally focused internally. Take that energy and spend more time in the customer's business before investing too much in new tactics or strategies.

HISTORY

This section is all about the idea that if we can learn from past efforts, we'll grow faster than if we're always re-inventing growth efforts. Score 13-16 and your company is built on habits that will lead to rapid learning from past effort. Growth will be faster and less expensive. Score 9-12 and you have some things in place, but chances are you need to plan both success and failure a little more before starting any new tactics. Score under 9 and we suggest doing more research into agile growth strategies and teaching your people how to think about rapid testing of growth tactics.

STRATEGY

This section focuses on your company's internal strategic planning processes. Are you more strategic or are you more planning oriented. Growth, by its nature, is in the future. It relies more on strategy than past performance. If you score 17-20, you have a future orientation and can rapidly re-adjust strategies as you learn more. If you score 12-16, you're relying on the past more than inventing a future. Work on getting rapid strategy in place. If you score under 11, teach your people the difference between strategy and planning.

When we use this scoring system with our prospects, we've found that high scores in both structure and temperament are our best indicator for how quickly the project's results are going to show up. If we're working with a low structure score and low temperament score, we build in extra time and expense because we've learned that even growth tactics that have worked like magic for a very similar organization will take a little more to work with a low scoring company.

If you have questions or want to know why we've set up the Growth Formula the way we did, please contact us via email or by reaching us at GoLeads.com. We're happy to share what we've learned and listen to stories of success or troubleshoot challenges.

Thank you for reading.

ABOUT THE AUTHORS

William Mattern is the President and CEO of GoLeads/USFarmData, a company he founded, owns, and has managed the past 18 years. A native of Nebraska, he lives in Omaha with his wife and three children and still loves all Big Red sports. This is his first booklet.

Greg Chambers is the President of Chambers Pivot Industries, a sales and marketing consulting company in Omaha, NE. A serial entrepreneur, Chambers co-founded GoLeads, founded Mad Gringo apparel, in addition to his consultancy. He is the author of the *AMALGAMATE: A mix of business* ideas booklets, the novel *The Legend of Mad Gringo*, and the soon to be published *The Human Being's Guide to Business Growth*, which can all be found on Amazon. His weekly *Right FIT Newsletter* is read by thousands of subscribers each week. You can find out more about Greg at chamberspivot.com.

www.ingramcontent.com/pod-product-compliance
Lightning Source LLC
Chambersburg PA
CBHW041115180526
45172CB00001B/262